ALERTING KIDS TO THE DANGER OF
ABUSE AND NEGLECT

WRITTEN BY JOY BERRY
Pictures by Bartholomew

WORD

Educational Products Division
Waco, Texas 76796

Executive Producer: Ron Berry
Producer: Marilyn Berry
Designer: Abigail Johnston
Contributing Editors: Nancy Cochran, Susan Motycka
Editor: Kate Dickey
Consultants: Ellen Klarberg, Kathleen McBride

Printed in the United States of America

ISBN: 0-8499-8224-3

Attention Parents and Teachers

What you don't know CAN hurt you!
People used to believe that children should be kept ignorant for their own sake. In our rapidly changing world, this simply isn't realistic any more. Your children need to know as much as they can about life and its **danger zones.** Since their imaginations can create fantasies worse than any actual situation, they need correct and comprehensible information. The more children know, the better they will be able to protect themselves should they encounter a dangerous situation.

All responsible, caring adults want children to be safe. Unfortunately, our society is becoming increasingly unsafe for children. Young people are being physically abused and neglected in alarming numbers. Recent statistics estimate that approximately one million cases of abuse and neglect occur in the United States each year. These incidents cut across all socioeconomic barriers.

Not all people who abuse and neglect children are primary caretakers. Indeed, many cases of abuse and neglect occur in schools, day care centers, camps, baby sitters' homes, and other "safe" places.

Parents can no longer feel that their kids are safe because neither parent is abusive or neglectful. Their children can be well cared for at home and abused or neglected away from home.

What can you do to help prevent these senseless and abhorrent incidents? Give your children the information they need to recognize abuse and neglect. This book provides simple explanations that children can understand. It tells children what they can do if they or a friend has been abused or neglected.

Read this book with your children and make sure they understand it. Ask them if they have any questions. Then answer their questions openly and honestly. By doing these things, you are taking an essential step toward ensuring your children's well-being. Their awareness of the problem and what to do about it can be their best protection.

The back of this book contains important information for parents and teachers. This section includes safety guidelines that you can follow to help protect your children.

This material is not intended to frighten you or your children. The point of this book is to turn fear into healthy caution and to empower young people to remain safe, happy, and free.

People from birth to
seventeen years of age
are called **minors.**
People eighteen years
of age and older
are called **adults.**

I'm a
minor.

Adults, such as
- parents,
- guardians,
- teachers,
- counselors, and
- baby sitters,
are responsible for the minors in their care.

Adults who are responsible for minors
must make sure that the minors
  • do not hurt themselves,
  • do not hurt other people, and
  • do not damage or destroy anyone's property.

When minors hurt themselves, adults are often responsible for seeing that they receive proper care.

He fell on the basketball court.

When minors hurt other people, adults must often take responsibility for seeing that the other people receive proper care.

When minors damage or destroy something,
adults must often take responsibility
for repairing or replacing it.

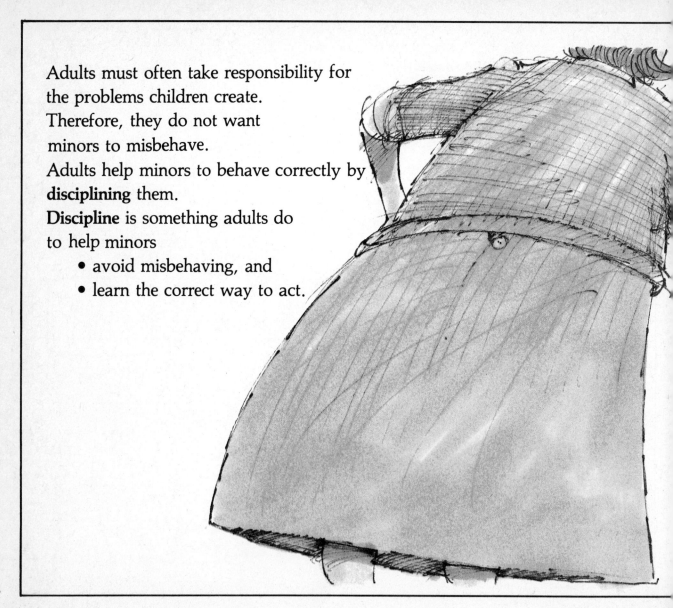

Adults must often take responsibility for
the problems children create.
Therefore, they do not want
minors to misbehave.
Adults help minors to behave correctly by
disciplining them.
Discipline is something adults do
to help minors

- avoid misbehaving, and
- learn the correct way to act.

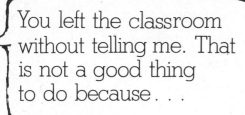

You left the classroom without telling me. That is not a good thing to do because. . .

Talking is one kind of discipline. Sometimes adults talk to minors and tell them what they should and should not do.
They also explain what will happen if minors misbehave.

Natural consequences are another kind of discipline. Some adults allow minors to suffer the consequences of their misbehavior. They let minors experience the bad things that happen automatically to them when they do something wrong. This helps minors to learn why they should not misbehave.

Inflicted consequences are another kind of discipline.
Some adults have minors do something they
do not like to do when they misbehave.
This is done so they will be sorry for misbehaving.

Since you broke your sister's toy, you'll have to replace it with your own money.

11

Isolation is another kind of discipline.
Some adults have minors go to places where
they will be alone so they will stop misbehaving.

Deprivation is another kind of discipline.
Some adults may not allow minors to do or
have something they enjoy when they misbehave.
This is done so they will be sorry for misbehaving.

Because you disobeyed me,
you may not watch TV today.

Physical punishment is another kind of discipline.
Some adults cause minors to feel
some kind of pain when they misbehave.
This is done so they will be sorry for misbehaving.
Spanking is one kind of physical punishment.

I'm afraid you deserved that one.

Most adults discipline children through
- talking,
- natural consequences,
- inflicted consequences,
- isolation,
- deprivation, or
- physical punishment.

Adults do these things to help minors
- avoid misbehaving, and
- learn the correct way to act.

Some adults overdo it
when they **discipline** minors.
They go too far and do too much.
The result is that they hurt minors
instead of helping them.

16

You're NO GOOD! You can't do anything right. I wish you'd never been born.

Some adults overdo it when they **talk** to minors. They talk very loudly or say extremely cruel things. Sometimes they do this in front of others. The things they say cause minors to

- be afraid most of the time,
- feel bad about everything they do,
- feel bad about themselves, and
- think they are incapable of doing anything good.

17

Some adults overdo it with **natural consequences.** They allow minors to suffer the consequences of their mistakes even when the consequences will severely hurt the minors.

It serves him right. He should know better than to play in the street. Let him learn the hard way.

Some adults overdo it with **inflicted consequences.**
They force minors to do things that are much
too difficult or too painful for minors.

Some adults overdo it when they **isolate** minors.
They make minors stay in frightening places
for very long periods of time.

It's scary being locked in this closet. They always make me stay in here for such a long time. I need to go to the bathroom.

SNiFF SNiFF

20

Some adults overdo it when they **deprive** minors. They take important things, such as food and water, away from minors, or they do not allow minors to do things that are necessary for their survival.

I'm so hungry. I haven't had anything to eat for two days.

You don't deserve to eat. You've been a bad boy.

Some adults overdo it when they **inflict punishment** on minors. They do things that cause
- bleeding,
- bruises,
- burns, or
- broken bones.

When adults overdo it, they are not disciplining minors.
They are **abusing** them. There are different kinds of abuse.
Anything that is done on purpose to cause illness, injury, or death
is called **physical abuse.**
Anything that causes a minor to feel very bad <u>all of the time</u>
is called **emotional abuse.**

Another kind of abuse is called **neglect**.
Neglect happens when adults fail to give minors
the things they need to survive and grow.

I'm worried about Tom. He never brings lunch or lunch money to school.

He's so thin. I'm sure he doesn't get enough food at home, either . . .

Some adults neglect minors by failing to give them **necessities,** such as
- food,
- clothing, and
- an adequate place to live.

Some adults neglect minors by failing to give them the **care** they need to stay healthy and well. These adults do not do anything to prevent minors from getting sick. Neither do they give minors the proper medical attention when they are sick or injured.

Some adults neglect minors by failing to give them the **supervision** they need to be safe. These adults do not try to keep minors from hurting themselves. Neither do they try to protect minors from possible harm.

This child was playing in the street. I almost hit her with my car.

Don't bother looking for her parents. They're never home. She stays alone most of the time.

Some adults neglect minors by failing to give them necessary **educational opportunities.** These adults prevent minors from participating in activities that would enable the minors to learn and grow mentally.

Your child hasn't been in school. Are you teaching him at home?

He does not have time for school. He has to work.

Some adults neglect minors by failing to give them the **social experiences** they need. These adults do not allow minors to talk to or be around others. Thus, the minors do not learn how to get along with other people.

There are many reasons why adults abuse and neglect minors.

1. IMMATURITY

Some adults are immature and lack the wisdom to behave correctly. This may result in their abusing and neglecting minors.

2. IGNORANCE

Some adults do not know very much about minors.
They do not know what minors need.
They do not know how to treat minors.
These adults become abusive and neglectful
because they do not know better.

Even though I have four children, I don't know how to raise them. No one ever taught me.

3. UNREALISTIC EXPECTATIONS
Some adults expect minors to act like adults. They do not realize that minors are not physically or mentally able to do this. When minors do not act grown up, the adults are often disappointed and become abusive or neglectful.

4. FRUSTRATION

Some adults are continually faced
with experiences they cannot handle.
They become frustrated.
Sometimes they need an outlet
for their frustration.
The outlet might be the abuse or
neglect of a minor.

5. UNFULFILLED NEEDS

Some adults do not feel that others
love or care about them.
They expect minors to love
or take care of them.
When minors cannot do these things,
the adults are often angry and
become abusive or neglectful.

No one takes care
of me, so why
should I take
care of anyone?

6. FEELING OVERWHELMED

Some adults do not have any family or friends living near them. These adults feel that there is no one to help them when they need it. They feel stranded and overwhelmed. These feelings often cause them to be abusive or neglectful.

7. DRUGS AND ALCOHOL

Some adults drink too much alcohol or take too many drugs.
The alcohol or drugs cause them to behave strangely.
This often includes abusing or neglecting minors.

OH, NO! He's going to get drunk again. He always hits me when he's drunk.

BRING ME
A BEER!

8. ABUSE AND NEGLECT

Some adults were abused or neglected
when they were minors.

This may affect them in one of two ways:

- They may think that abuse and neglect
  are OK because that is what they
  experienced when they were minors, or
- They may be angry and want to get
  back at someone for the abuse and
  neglect they experienced as minors.

There are many reasons why some adults are abusive and neglectful. These reasons, however, do not justify their behavior. Abuse and neglect are **WRONG**.

It is **AGAINST THE LAW** for **ANY** adult
to abuse **ANY** minor for **ANY** reason.

This law applies to all
- parents,
- guardians,
- relatives,
- teachers,
- camp counselors,
- baby sitters,
- friends,
- neighbors, and
- strangers.

It is **AGAINST THE LAW** for **ANY** adult
to neglect **ANY** minor who is in his or her care.

It is **AGAINST THE LAW** for **YOU**
to be abused or neglected.

No matter who you are or what you have done,
you should <u>never</u> be
- abused physically,
- abused emotionally, or
- neglected.

Sometimes it is hard to know
whether or not an adult
has actually abused or neglected you.
It is hard to tell
the difference between
discipline and abuse.
It is also hard to tell
the difference between
what you think you need and
what you actually need.
It is especially hard
for you to decide
these things by yourself.

How do we know whether
or not we have been
abused or neglected?

Caring adults can help you.

There is <u>always someone</u> who can help you determine whether or not you have been abused or neglected.

Talk to someone if you feel that
an adult is abusing or neglecting you.
Choose a person you trust.
Make sure it is someone who is old enough and
wise enough to help you.
It might be
- a parent,
- a guardian,
- a teacher,
- a principal,
- a minister,
- a close relative
  (such as a grandparent, aunt, or uncle), or
- an adult friend.

Make sure you tell the truth.
Do not keep back any of the details
of what has happened.
Do not exaggerate.
Telling the truth in these situations
is extremely important.

. . . and that's
the truth!

If the adult you are concerned about
has not actually abused or neglected you,
the people you talk to can assure you of that fact.
They can also help you understand why
the adult behaved that way.

Making you go to your room is not really abusive. . . it sounds more like discipline.

Good point.

If you have been abused or neglected,
the people you talk to can get help for you and
make sure that the abuse or neglect does not continue.

The people who help you may need to separate you
for a period of time from the adult who has
abused or neglected you.

This separation allows the adult
to pay attention to solving the problems
that are causing the abuse or neglect.
It also allows you to feel safe and receive proper care.

If you think a friend is being abused or neglected,
encourage your friend to talk to caring adults.
You may also want to talk to adults about the situation
to make sure that your friend gets help.

If the adults you talk to don't help you, talk to other adults.
Keep talking to people until you find someone to help you.

No one should ever be
- physically abused,
- emotionally abused, or
- neglected.

THIS INCLUDES YOU!

Providing a Safe Environment For Your Children

Be careful when you select the adults who spend time with your children (baby sitters, teachers, counselors, etc.). Choose people who are caring, competent, and responsible.

To help you determine whether or not a person is qualified to spend time with your children, do the following:

- Interview the person.
- Observe the person in action.
- Talk to people who know the person.
- Have your children spend time with the person.
- Have your children help you decide whether or not they should get involved with the person.

Be careful when you select the programs that your children participate in. Make sure that day care centers and schools are licensed by the state and meet legal requirements regarding

- supervision,
- enrollment,
- indoor space,
- outdoor space,
- facilities,
- play equipment and materials,
- activities,
- schedule, and
- discipline.

Do the following before you get your children involved in a program:

- Observe and find out everything you can about the program.
- Talk to other people who are or have been involved in the program.
- Allow your children to observe the program.
- Have your children help you decide whether or not they should participate in the program.

Once you enroll your children, observe or participat the program as often as possible so that you will k whether or not it is maintaining its quality and effec ness.

Common Signs of Abuse and Neglect

Extreme Behavior

Children who are abused or neglected might bec overly

- aggressive,
- disruptive,
- destructive,
- affectionate (with everyone, including strangers)
- withdrawn,
- passive, or
- shy.

Unusual Appearance

Children who are abused or neglected might

- wear dirty, tattered, or torn clothes,
- dress inappropriately for the weather,
- lack good personal hygiene, or
- look undernourished.

Children who are abused might also be overly dresse overly neat. Their parents, in an effort to gain con might be imposing unrealistic standards of perfectio them.

Medical Problems

Children who are abused or neglected may

- have repeated injuries,
- be ill frequently,
- have poor dental health, or
- not receive the medical attention that most chil receive (eye examinations, immunizations, etc.).